The Road of Life
and other poems

The Road of Life
and other poems

Barbara May Boot

ATHENA PRESS
LONDON

The Road of Life
and other poems
Copyright © Barbara May Boot 2010

All Rights Reserved

No part of this book may be reproduced in any form
by photocopying or by any electronic or mechanical means,
including information storage or retrieval systems,
without permission in writing from both the copyright
owner and the publisher of this book.

ISBN 978 1 84748 808 4

First published 2010 by
ATHENA PRESS
Queen's House, 2 Holly Road
Twickenham TW1 4EG
United Kingdom

Printed for Athena Press

To my husband John, my daughters Sue and Carol and my grandchildren James and Emily.

Contents

The Crown Green Bowling Match	9
A Game of Scrabble	11
A Walk Along the Beach	13
Grandma's Special Teapot	15
The M25 Motorway	17
The Church at Applecross	18
Beautiful Scotland	20
Our Feathered Friends of the Garden	22
Taking Things for Granted	23
Our Ladies' Choir	24
A Country Walk	26
A World Without Music	28
Memories	30
Ben	32
Our Senses	34
The Road of Life	36
The Old Rustic Bench	37
The Old Rocking Chair	39

Passing By	41
Tomorrow	43
A Walk in the Garden	45
The Mystery of Life	47
The Artist	48
The Trials and Jubilations of Singing in a Choir	49
Smile	51
Give Away a Smile	52
Holidays	54
A Visit to the Doctor's	55
A Day With a Vet	56
The Golden Years	58
Ages	59
Friendship	60
There is a Hymn	62
The Twilight Years	63
Requests	64
What Easter Means to You	65
My Christmas Card Address Book	66
What was Christmas Like for you?	67
Christmas is Here	69
What does Christmas mean to you?	71

The Crown Green Bowling Match

The men and ladies were ready to play,
As they stood on the edge of the green;
Full of anticipation of the game,
Feeling confident and serene.

It was quite a pleasant morning,
As they watched the players arrive.
They got out of their cars walking slowly,
Looking glad to be alive.

The opposition looked very determined,
As they removed the bowls from their holders,
Put the correct shoes on their feet
And threw a towel over their shoulders.

Everything was ready, so play began;
The jack was sent at a steady pace.
'That's gone a long way,' the player said,
With a determined look on his face.

With four people playing each end,
The bowls ended up very near.
So a measure was needed to sort it out,
They all stood around with great fear.

After the measure was taken,
They still couldn't decide who had won.
'We will call it a draw,' the captain said,
So that was decided upon.

The match ended up very close,
Just a few points separated each team.
They all agreed it had been quite fun,
A good way for letting off steam.

A Game of Scrabble

A game of Scrabble can be
Thrilling and brain-teasing;
Trying to make the longest word you can,
With letters that are not pleasing.

You try to outwit your opponent
By using your best tiles,
Make a seven-letter word
To boost your score by miles.

Z and Q are worth ten points,
J and X are eight.
Use them to increase your score,
Be patient and just wait.

The highest total on the board
Is when you use the triple.
Use these for your highest tiles
And let your senses ripple.

You can play Scrabble
Anywhere you are.
On the train or in a plane
Or even in the car.

Scrabble comes in all sizes –
Deluxe or very small,
Travel games in a little box,
But the computer's best of all.

You can all play Scrabble
With two, three or four,
The object of the game, you see,
Is to get the highest score.

A Walk Along the Beach

The sun is making the sea sparkle
As along the beach I walk.
It is so very peaceful,
I hardly dare to talk.

My feet are making patterns
In the soft brown sand;
The seagulls fly along the shore,
Then on the rocks they land.

The tide is just on the ebb,
Slowly coming into the bay,
As children make their sandcastles,
On the beach for just a day.

I sit among the rock pools,
Seaweed clings among the gloom.
The little pools are so shallow
There is hardly any room.

Among the little rocks I find
Pretty seashells pink and small.
The oystercatchers take to the air,
With their distinctive call.

The rocks are now quite big,
A bit further along the beach;
The waves crash up and over them,
They are very hard to reach.

I have had a lovely day,
Walking by the sea.
The sun is sinking in the sky
So I must go home for tea.

Grandma's Special Teapot

When I was just a little girl,
I can remember it well,
Grandma's special teapot,
It was shaped just like a bell.

This large bell-shaped teapot
Was very special indeed,
With leaves and coloured flowers,
Patterns of red and white tweed.

This very special teapot
Was getting very old.
It would not keep the tea warm
So your drink was always cold.

'This will not do,' Granny said,
'We cannot have cold tea.'
So she put the teapot on a shelf,
For everyone to see.

The years passed by so quickly,
The teapot looked so sad,
Sitting on that lonely shelf,
Looking dismal and not glad.

Then one day it happened:
A wedding was taking place
So the teapot was needed,
No more was it in disgrace.

The teapot was carefully washed,
Making it look quite pretty.
Placed on the table at the wedding feast,
While the guests sang a merry ditty.

The teapot was no longer on the shelf
Where it had stood for years.
Its pretty colours freshly renewed,
Feeling glad and full of cheer.

The M25 Motorway

Have you ever travelled
On the M25 motorway?
It is quite an experience,
This, I can truly say.

Some people say this motorway
Resembles a great car park,
If this dilemma you wish to avoid
You will need to get up with the lark.

The road is very busy,
With lorries, cars and trucks.
But the scenery's quite pleasant,
No need to read your books.

As you travel along this road,
You are linked to numerous towns.
Making some journeys very easy,
Banishing all your groans or frowns.

As you travel along this road
You pass near the airport,
With planes flying very low,
It can make your nerves feel fraught.

You need to be quite careful,
Make sure your route is sound.
Because the road is circular,
You could keep on going round.

The Church at Applecross

There is a church at Applecross,
So simple and surreal.
Quiet and very peaceful,
It has a magnetic feel.

There is nothing grand
About this little place.
But a feeling of sincerity
Will just light up your face.

There are no stained-glass windows
Or a regal altar stone,
But a simple wooden table
Standing all alone.

As you step through the door,
Just a vestibule greets you,
With stairs up in the corner,
To a balcony with a view.

The walls are thick and solid.
The stones are painted white.
No flashy drapes or paintings –
A pleasant, lovely sight.

The preacher's lectern is
Up some little stairs,
Where he can see the people
Who come to say their prayers.

What is such a delight
About this little church
Is the peace and quiet
Within your heart to search.

It was so lovely sitting there,
That beautiful summer's day.
On old chairs with straight-up backs,
Beautiful memories to stay.

Beautiful Scotland

Have you ever been to Scotland
With its mountainous terrain?
No matter what people tell you,
It doesn't always rain.

You can travel along single roads,
With many passing places.
Grazing, rough highland cows
With cute woolly faces.

The lochs are calm and bountiful,
Surrounded by hills and trees.
Every corner you may turn
Reveals a different view to please.

Then there are the sunsets,
A different one each night,
The colours are amazing,
It's such a beautiful sight.

The happy Scottish people
Are so jolly and genteel,
With their distinctive accent
And their sincerity so real.

They play the bagpipes with gusto
And dance the Highland fling.
The music is so merry,
You want to clap and sing.

The waterfalls are many,
The mountains are so high –
You can hardly see the tops,
As they reach into the sky.

If you have some time to spare,
Go and take a visit.
You will be made most welcome,
It really is exquisite.

Our Feathered Friends of the Garden

Collared doves come in pairs,
Cooing and romancing.
White-grey wood pigeons
Look as though they are dancing.

Robins with their bright redbreast
Feed upon the seeds,
Taking only what they want
For their daily needs.

Then there are the magpies,
Swooping down in haste.
They frighten the other birds away,
None can match their pace.

The little hedge sparrow
Is such a delight to see,
Hopping from branch to branch
As it climbs the old plum tree.

The most popular birds we see
Are blackbirds young and old,
They like to feed on bread,
Whether it is warm or cold.

We like to feed our garden birds,
They give us so much pleasure.
One of nature's sheer delights,
A thing for us to treasure.

Taking Things for Granted

The baker's on strike again today,
We have no bread for tea.
The dustbin men did not come,
Our dustbins are as full as can be.

The paperboy was rather late,
My comic did not arrive.
The early bus did not start out,
The driver too tired to drive.

I have a hole in my shoe,
It will need a special repair.
I would take it to the cobblers,
But the shop is no longer there.

I was feeling rather ill,
So a doctor I needed to see.
I trundled along as best I could,
But the doctor had gone to tea.

I had a pleasant swim last week;
I will go again today.
When I arrived the pool was closed,
No attendant there to pay.

These things we take for granted,
But when they are not there,
We place the blame on others
For the state of the world that we share.

Our Ladies' Choir

We are a ladies' choir
Who like to sing a lot
And come to practise every week,
At ten-thirty on the dot.

We are quite a motley bunch,
Happy and quite merry,
Especially behind the conductor's back
When we pass around the sherry.

The contraltos sing very low,
The sopranos sing up high.
But if we ever get it wrong
We are greeted with a sigh.

Our elderly conductor,
Who is a very sprightly man,
Keeps us all in order
Whenever he possibly can.

Our pianist is very good,
Her fingers are so agile.
As up and down the keys she plays,
It really makes you smile.

When we do our breathing,
We have to stand up straight.
Then we sing the various scales –
It makes you feel really great.

Christmas time is very special,
Our carols we like to sing.
So we go and visit the elderly
With our Christmas message to bring.

If you are feeling unhappy,
Just sing a jolly song.
Singing is very good for you,
You'll not feel sad for long.

A Country Walk

I want you all to picture
A sunny country walk
By green and grassy meadows
With poppies on slender stalks.

The sky is blue, the sun is hot,
It's such a pleasant morn,
As we wander by the meadow,
Passing fields of waving corn.

In the distance a church we see,
With a steeple tall and straight.
There's a little group of people
Passing through the old lychgate.

We stand a while and listen
To the cuckoo's distinctive call
And watch the cheeky blackbird
In a leafy tree so tall.

A little stream runs by our path,
Boulders green with moss.
There are tumbling waterfalls
And a bridge for us to cross.

In the distance we can hear
The farmer sowing his seeds,
As up and down the field he ploughs
Planting grain for all our needs.

We have followed the country path
Using our mind's eye.
I'm sure you can imagine it too
If you just sit back and try.

A World Without Music

What a dull place the world would be
If there was not any music.
How quiet and sad our lives would be
If there was not any music.

Just imagine going to church
Having no hymns to sing.
How quiet the village churches would be
If the bells had no music to ring.

No evening song from the birds again
As in the garden we walk.
Everywhere is so deathly quiet,
We hardly dare to talk.

But I'm glad to say this is not so,
There is plenty of music to hear.
Whether at home or in the concert hall,
Happy tunes make us cheer.

There is no need to feel sad,
Unhappy or downhearted.
Just whistle a merry tune
When each new day has started.

We can sing our hymns in church
And hear the organ play,
Because composers have written
The music we hear today.

So to everyone I beg you
Let music fill your heart.
It blows away the grey clouds
As each new day we start.

Memories

Do you remember
When you were small
And the old tin bath
Hung on the lavatory wall?

Do you remember
The walk to the loo,
Down the backyard
Even when you were two?

Do you remember
The old dolly tub
Which Mum used on Monday
The washing to rub?

Do you remember
Before the telly came,
We'd listen to the wireless?
Dick Barton again!

Do you remember
The ration books too –
Queuing for ages
For a plate of lamb stew?

Do you remember
The black-leaded grate
That always needed cleaning
No matter how late?

Do you remember
The milkman's horse?
Or the man with the coal
In sacks rough and coarse?

Do you remember
Dad's very first car?
When you travelled in style
You felt like a star.

Do you remember
In the shelters at night,
When the bombers flew over
How they gave us a fright?

These are just thoughts
As we think of the past.
Nothing can replace them,
Our memories will last.

Ben

My name is Ben, I'm only a pup,
My coat is cream, my eyes are mellow.
But all in all I think you could say
I'm a very happy little fellow.

When I was just a few weeks old,
With a family I went to stay.
They taught me how to do things right
In a proper doggie way.

There were lots of different things to learn,
Like walking on a lead
And knowing when to 'sit' and 'stay'
Whenever there was a need.

When I was one I went to live
At a centre to be trained,
To cross the road with safety –
Even when it rained!

When my training's over
I am going to be
A friend and a companion
To someone who cannot see.

I'll use my eyes to guide them
Around life's difficult ways.
With obstacles and dangers,
In these uncertain days.

My life will be a happy one,
Guiding my friend along.
I'll use the gift God gave me,
He'll help me to be strong.

Our Senses

Did you hear the cuckoo
From a distant tree,
Or the crashing of the waves
In a very, very rough sea?

Did you see the rainbow
In the sky so bright,
Or the fledgling blackbird
Taking his first flight?

Did you smell the perfume
Of the flowers after rain,
Or the sooty coal dust
From a very old steam train?

Did you taste the citrus tang
From a juicy lemon,
Or the sweet and sickly flavour
You get only from a melon?

Did you touch the soft fur
On a puppy or a kitten,
Or the warm feel of wool
From your winter mitten?

All of these senses
You possibly possess,
But if we ever lose them
It causes some distress.

Did you hear the church bells
Ringing in the steeple,
Or the chattering of voices
In a room full of people?

Did you see the little bud
Open into a flower,
Or the droplets on a petal
After the first spring shower?

Did you smell the aroma
Of freshly home-baked bread,
Or the woody air of fallen leaves
As through the woods you tread?

Did you taste the saltiness
From your fish and chips,
Or the chocolate and marshmallow
You get from walnut whips?

Did you touch the hand
Of a newborn child,
Or snuggle up in bed at night
In sheets all soft and mild?

Let us all be thankful
For the senses we can use
And not feel too downhearted
About the ones we sometimes lose.

The Road of Life

Life is like a winding road,
With many twists and turns.
Yet a road is planned and surveyed,
While life is something we must learn.

Going down a road for the first time,
Compare it with starting school,
You feel a bit apprehensive,
Not knowing the golden rule.

We now have reached some roadmen,
What career would you advise?
With cautionary lights at the roadworks,
It pays to plan and be wise.

There's a hill ahead so beware!
Your next choice in life could be deadly.
At the top of the hill is a downward slope,
Maybe marriage is not that friendly.

We are coming to some crossroads,
Life's slowing down a bit now.
Which way do we go at the junction?
Perhaps you could tell me how.

You cannot see the future,
Like you can't see round a bend.
Perhaps that's what life is all about,
Its mysteries never end.

The Old Rustic Bench

In our garden beneath a tree,
There's a bench, rustic and old,
Where people could just sit awhile
When the weather's warm or cold.

The children can imagine
It is a galleon of old,
Where vagabonds and pirates
Fight soldiers strong and bold.

Another time the bench might be
A fort of long ago,
With cowboys and Red Indians
Fighting with arrows and a bow.

I remember when the bench was new,
Carefully placed beneath the tree,
What a joy it was to sit and rest
In perfect harmony.

The bench has seen many changes,
While standing beneath that tree.
Both young and old have sat content
While enjoying a cup of tea.

With the difference of each season,
The bench took on a different glow.
From the bright and sunny summer,
To the winter's coat of snow.

The bench still stands beneath the tree,
The children grown and gone.
Perhaps one day they will return,
To the bench they once sat on.

The Old Rocking Chair

An old lady by the fireside sits
In an old wooden rocking chair
And remembers the days of long ago,
About a girl with raven-black hair.

She recalls the days at the village school,
Where lessons were scribbled on a slate.
The teachers were tall and very strict;
You knew you must never be late.

The fun and games in the playground,
You played with a top, a hoop or ball,
But playing kiss chase with the boys –
That was the best game of all.

On Sunday she would go to church,
Up the hill in a pony and trap,
In her lace bonnet and Sunday dress,
Ankle boots tied with a strap.

The little old lady slumbers awhile,
A smile on her wrinkled face,
As she thinks of the very busy past,
But life's now a much slower pace.

On waking up, her thoughts return
To her childhood long ago.
Then came the dreamy teenage years,
When she courted her favourite beau.

The rocking chair starts to slowly rock,
As the old lady quietly sighs,
Causing the rhythmic movement
So peaceful, she closes her eyes.

The rocking chair on the hearth still stands,
The old lady long since gone.
Maybe she will return some day;
Until then her memory lives on.

Passing By

It was always on a Tuesday
The old lady went down the road.
She was a creature of habit,
Whether it was warm or cold.

It was always on a Tuesday
The old man went down the road.
He was a creature of habit,
Walking tall and bold.

As down the road they walked,
Passing each other by,
Each with their own special thoughts,
Perhaps a little shy.

This pair of lonely people,
Never dared to even speak,
When they trundled to and from the shop
On Tuesday every week.

Then one day it happened,
They caught each other's eye.
It was a pleasant Tuesday,
With the sun up in the sky.

It happened again the following week –
They caught each other's eye –
But also a smile was exchanged,
As they were passing by.

With confidence their glances grew,
As each week passed with pleasure,
They began to accept each Tuesday
Was a time for them to treasure.

The weeks passed by so quickly,
As down the road they walked.
Then the inevitable happened,
They stopped to have a talk.

Going down the road on Tuesday,
With the sun up in the sky,
Now they walk together
Instead of passing by.

Tomorrow

I hear Mrs Smith is ill again,
Should I send a card,
Or a get-well refrain?
Perhaps I will, tomorrow!

My neighbour has broken his arm
I think I'll bake him a cake,
That can do him no harm,
Perhaps I will, tomorrow!

My friend telephoned the other day,
I should ring her back
I know we both have plenty to say.
Perhaps I will, tomorrow!

I received a letter some time ago,
A letter in return I must write.
It will give them pleasure I know,
Perhaps I will, tomorrow!

The lawns are growing longer,
The windows, they need cleaning.
But first I must feel stronger,
Perhaps I will, tomorrow!

When at the Pearly Gates we stand,
We ask the Lord to let us in.
For we believe it's the Promised Land,
He answers, 'Perhaps I will, tomorrow!'

But as you know there's no tomorrow,
So through life you should say,
Forget tomorrow,
Say, 'Yes, I'll do it today.'

A Walk in the Garden

When you go walking in the garden,
What is the first thing you see?
Growing around in lovely colours,
Are flowers in profusion all around me.

Have you ever stopped to marvel
At the beauty of a flower,
Or the glistening raindrops
At the end of every shower?

The pink and white of blossom time,
As each springtime is renewed,
To be followed by the autumn fruits,
Giving birds their winter food.

Gardens are a special place,
With nature in abundance.
Where you can sit and rest awhile
While listening to the silence.

In wintertime the garden
Can lose its natural glow,
But what a transformation
After a heavy fall of snow.

Nature is a wonder
That we can all embrace.
We can work in the garden
Or enjoy the open space.

There are so many lovely flowers
Around the world for us to see.
They lift our spirits when we are sad
And fill our homes with ecstasy.

Next time you go walking in a garden,
Take special notice of the flowers there.
Then you will also stop to marvel
At the beauty we all can share.

The Mystery of Life

We don't all get a chance in life
To make our lives anew,
When we can set aside our past
And plan the future too.

Sometimes life's an uphill struggle,
When everything you do goes wrong.
That's when you need some extra courage,
To show the world you are strong.

As we travel along life's way,
We have our ups and downs.
Somehow we will come smiling through,
Forgetting our doubts and frowns.

When you get up each morning,
Plan your day from morn till night.
Buy yourself a bunch of flowers,
They always make the home look bright.

At the moment life may seem
Full of toil and sorrow.
Try and find the brighter side,
There'll always be tomorrow.

Although tomorrow never comes
And your life feels dull,
Try to wear a happy smile –
Live life to the full.

The Artist

The artist sat at his easel,
Looking at the blank canvas there,
No artistic thoughts could he muster,
He could only sit and stare.

He picked up his nearest paintbrush,
Then dabbed it in some paint,
Scrawled some lines on the canvas,
Some thick, some very faint.

He stood and looked at the canvas,
Some shape was taking place.
So he added some more brushstrokes
And started to fill in the space.

He then added some colour,
Blue, yellow, green and gold.
These brightened up the painting,
Making it warm and bold.

Every so often the artist
Stood back to admire his picture,
He looked at the lines and definition
His heart had managed to capture.

When the artist had finished,
The painting was a glorious sight
Of trees, lakes and mountains,
Letting in the sun's beautiful light.

The Trials and Jubilations of Singing in a Choir

'We are going to give a concert,'
The choirmaster told the choir.
'We'll invite our friends and relations,
So a hall we need to hire.'

It was duly decided,
A time and date was chosen.
'We will have it in the spring time,
Then the roads will not be frozen.'

They had a little discussion
About what songs to sing.
Perhaps some a little sombre,
But most with a happy swing.

Perhaps we could invite
A soloist to take part
And add their special talent,
To create a happy start.

The tickets were all printed
And the programmes too.
It really was a busy time
With such a lot to do.

The concert is now over,
I am sure it was enjoyed by all
Who came to listen to the choir,
They really had a ball.

I bet you did not realise
Singing stimulates the brain.
So if you're feeling sad and low,
Let singing take the strain.

If you can sing a little bit,
Then you could join a choir,
Provided you can reach the notes
As they gradually get higher.

But if singing is not your forte,
Then come and hear us sing.
We'll make you feel so happy,
You will dance a Highland fling.

I am sure you will agree,
Your presence we require
To witness the trials and jubilations
Of singing in a choir.

Smile

When you got up this morning,
Did you say a little prayer,
To thank the Lord for this new day,
To show how much you care?

When you got up this morning,
Did you have a smile upon your face,
To show the world how happy you are
To be part of the human race?

It needs less muscles to make a smile,
Don't go around with a frown.
A smile puts a sparkle in your eye,
It lifts people who are down.

To give a smile is very easy,
Meet all your friends with a grin.
It only shows you're happy,
Their confidence to win.

It does not cost you money,
To give away a smile
To people while out shopping,
It makes life so worthwhile.

So when you get up tomorrow,
Start the day off with a smile,
To show the people around you,
You are ready to run that mile.

Give Away a Smile

Did you give your neighbour a smile
When you met her in the street?
Or cast your eyes to the ground
Not wanting her to greet.

Did you give the postman a smile
When he delivered your post?
Or just shut the door on him,
Not being the perfect host.

A smile is infectious,
I'm sure you will agree.
If I smile at you,
Then you will smile back at me.

It really is quite easy
To give away a smile.
They cost very little
And are so versatile.

What makes you feel happy,
A smile or a frown?
Sometimes we are sad,
And can feel quite down.

Just look in a mirror,
Give yourself a grin.
It will make you feel happy
As you pucker up your chin.

Next time you meet your neighbour,
Don't turn and run a mile,
Show you care about them
And give away a smile.

Holidays

We all enjoy our holidays,
In autumn, summer or spring.
We pack our bags and off we go,
Whatever the weather may bring.

The journey might not be very long,
Perhaps only a mile or two.
But it's the change that does you good
And fills us with vigour anew.

Sometimes we go on a special trip,
To lands across the sea.
Where time has stood still it seems,
Over the previous century.

There are lots of places to visit,
With mountains, rivers and falls,
Sandy beaches and tossing seas
Where hungry seagulls call.

So off we go on our holidays,
Our camera strapped to our backs,
Recording all the happy days,
As we walk the mountain tracks.

We all like sunny weather
And the rain makes everywhere green,
So enjoy your holiday
And relish the mountain scene.

A Visit to the Doctor's

We often need a doctor,
Whether we are young or old.
It could be painful chilblains
Or just a common cold.

The surgery is a happy place,
With doctors and the nurses,
Where you can bring your ailments
And all your many curses.

We only visit the doctor's
When we are feeling ill.
They listen to us quietly
Then cure us with a pill.

Because our bodies are intricate,
The doctor needs to know
About our different illnesses;
His sympathy he will show.

Little Johnnie's got an earache,
Young Lucy's hurt her toe.
So where do we take them?
To the doctor's we all go.

Nowadays the surgery
Is quite a busy place,
With all the different ailments
That affect the human race.

A Day With a Vet

The telephone rings
It's now two a.m.
'Farmer Giles here, vet –
It's happened again.'
I grope for my clothes,
My wellingtons too,
Drive up to the farm,
Wish I'd gone to the loo.
The farmer is waiting,
He is looking quite pale.
There's the poor old cow,
Looking mournful and frail.
I do what I can for that poor old cow,
Then stumble to bed
Goodness only knows how.

It's now ten a.m.
And surgery's due,
Here comes young Johnny
And Tiddles too.
'What's the matter with Tiddles on this fine
    day?'
'He's hurt his foot, I'm sad to say.'
'Let's have a look then, oh that's not too bad
I'll put on some cream,
That will make him feel glad.'

Here's old Mrs Green with Samson her dog,
If you ask me he looks more like a hog.
She says his ear is very sore
But before I could look,
He'd dashed out of the door.
'He doesn't like vets,'
Says old Mrs Green, she followed old Samson,
Never more to be seen.

When surgery's over there's no time for lunch
I'm off on my rounds, some biscuits I'll munch.
There's sheep and some cows and horses galore
Waiting for me at their stable door.
With a soft voice and my gentle hands,
I care for their needs, cuts or swollen glands.

The calls are all over so home I will travel
To relax by the fire and have a game of Scrabble.
By ten p.m. I'm so tired I just stumble to bed
And fall off to sleep feeling cosy and red.

The telephone rings, it's now two a.m.
'Farmer Giles here, vet –
It's happened again.'

The Golden Years

When you're first married,
It's like having a ball.
Two young hearts in love,
Walking straight and tall.

The first few years
Come and go in a flash.
But when the children arrive,
There never seems enough cash.

But you struggle along
With your wonderful brood,
They always cheer you up
When you are in a bad mood.

Years thirty and forty
Come and go in a daze.
But then you reach fifty,
That surely is praise.

For fifty is a milestone
You have reached together.
While caring and sharing
Life's wonderful pleasure.

Being married for fifty years
Is quite an endeavour.
Just sit back and reflect
On your memories together.

Ages

At the age of four or five
Your learning process begins.
So off to school you are sent,
Your mind is in a spin.

Between ten and twenty
Life is just beginning.
Your very first boyfriend,
With passion you are winning.

Years thirty and forty
Come and go in a spin.
With children to care for,
You cannot give in.

When you are fifty
Life starts slowing down,
The children are grown up,
But that's no course to frown.

Now you've reached sixty
That's the best time of all
For letting your hair down
And having a ball.

You can sit with your feet up
And not give a damn.
You don't have to worry
About pushing a pram.

Friendship

A friend is someone
Who is always by your side.
When you are in trouble,
They are your special guide.

A friend is a person
Who listens with care,
To your troubles and heartaches;
Your problems they will share.

A friend is a person
Who makes you smile,
When life is a struggle,
They go that extra mile.

A friend is someone
Who is there when you fall.
They encourage you to face life,
To walk straight and tall.

A friend stands by you
Along life's rocky way,
Sharing good and bad times,
Your friendship will always stay.

A friend is someone
Who is always willing
To assist in the little jobs
You often find unfulfilling.

If you have a friend,
Who is faithful and true,
Cherish the special moments,
All your life through.

There is a Hymn

There is a hymn to suit all moods,
Whether you are happy or sad.
With so many from which to choose,
You really should be glad.

There is a hymn which we sing
About Easter and Christ dying.
But then on every Easter morn,
We rejoice in Him reviving.

There is a hymn, no doubt you know,
Of harvest and wheat sowing.
When we like to decorate the church
With food that has been growing.

There is a hymn which was written by
A great man named Charles Wesley.
It is his family's birthday hymn
That tells of his life precisely.

There is a hymn we can join in
At Christmas time, rejoicing,
About the birth of Jesus Christ,
With all the choirs singing.

There are many lovely hymns
That are written still today,
For choirs and solo voices
That make us feel quite gay.

The Twilight Years

As we reach our twilight years,
Our past comes flooding back,
Of happy days long since gone,
Some faculties we may now lack.

In our twilight years
Our lives are slowing down.
But we have lots of memories,
So don't sit around with a frown.

Our legs are not so strong
To walk for mile and mile.
But we have a happy heart,
So greet each day with a smile.

Our hearing gets fainter,
Our eyesight too,
But our hearts are strong
And they will see us through.

Enjoy your twilight years,
There is no need to work,
Relax and take things easy,
That is life's little perk.

So as we are growing older,
Don't sit around shedding tears,
Be very glad you have reached
Those rewarding twilight years.

Requests

Did you do it with loving hands?
The job that you were given.
Did you enjoy it with a contented heart?
The job that you were given.

If a request is worth undertaking
And it gives you pleasure,
Do it with a happy heart,
The moments you will treasure.

If you are asked to do a job,
Don't do it feeling downhearted.
Tackle it with a happy mind,
You'll feel great before you have started.

You may never know
When your help is needed.
So always be ready
To tackle your task unheeded.

The request you are asked to do
Could be large or small,
It may take an hour or two,
Or really no time at all.

Next time someone says to you,
'Will you do a job for me?'
Don't grumble and say you have no time,
Say yes and do it with glee.

What Easter Means to You

Do you think of all the cruelty,
That happened on the cross,
The turmoil and the sorrow,
When Pilate showed who's boss?

All that noise and commotion
On that crowded hill.
People crying openly,
Some people feeling ill.

Can you possibly imagine
What it was really like
To be pushed and jostled by the crowd,
Then stuck upon a spike?

Do you think He was afraid
Of being prodded and made to walk
By the mean and burly soldiers,
So thirsty, He could not talk?

But Jesus we know rose again,
On that glorious Easter morn.
So our lives could be saved,
Not outcast and forlorn.

So lift your hearts at Easter,
Don't let your thoughts be sad
About what happened on that hill,
Rejoice and all be glad.

My Christmas Card Address Book

At Christmas time I have
A precious little book,
With a list of people I know,
So I go and have a look.

This list of people's names
Is quite a lengthy list
So I must be very careful,
That someone is not missed.

The collection of these names
I have had for many years.
Faces I still remember,
Some glad, some bring tears.

Not many on my Christmas list
Do I meet to have a talk,
Because they live so far away,
Certainly too far to walk.

Now this list of people
Is very dear to me,
I met them all in the past,
And these people I may never see.

So every Christmas when I write
Their names upon my card
I see their faces in my mind,
It really is not hard.

What was Christmas Like for you?

What was Christmas like for you
When you were just a child?
Perhaps a war was raging,
When you were just a child.

Mum and Dad did their best
To make our Christmas bright.
A pretty tree with candles on
Filled the house with shimmering light.

Was your stocking filled with presents,
When you were just a child?
Was the turkey stuffed with lemon stuffing,
When you were just a child?

Perhaps an apple or orange you received
When you were just a child,
Or a rag doll your mother made,
When you were just a child.

Was your Christmas happier
When you were just a child?
Times could be very cold and bleak,
When you were just a child.

Simple gifts gave lots of joy
When you were just a child.
A woolly hat with gloves to match
In case the wind was wild.

But nowadays the children want
Lots of presents galore.
They are never satisfied,
If gifts don't fill the floor.

So as Christmas approaches,
Let your memories run wild,
Back to the festive season
When you were just a child.

Christmas is Here

The tree is glowing with Christmas lights,
Pretty parcels lie underneath.
Christmas crackers are ready to pull,
On the door hangs a welcome wreath.

The turkey's cooked a golden brown,
With chestnut stuffing too.
The Christmas pudding is steaming hot,
Just right for me and you.

The house is warm and glowing bright,
With cards and decorations.
We've given gifts to friends old and new
And some to our relations.

This is the type of Christmas
We are hoping to enjoy.
But a very different Christmas
For a certain baby boy.

It happened a long time ago,
In a stable dark and cold.
This baby boy was born,
In Bethlehem we are told.

No clean white sheets or baby crib,
Just a manger full of hay,
Where Mary laid the little boy,
On our very first Christmas day.

So let us all remember,
As we enjoy our Christmas fare,
Baby Jesus from long ago
In a stable cold and bare.

What does Christmas mean to you?

What does Christmas mean to you,
Buying presents by the score,
Hanging glowing lights that shine,
Putting a wreath upon the door?

Sometimes we go carolling,
To people who are old.
We hope that they all enjoy it
Even though it might be cold.

Christmas means different things
To people young and old.
Children listen carefully,
While the Christmas stories are told.

No doubt you've bought some special food,
And your home will be nice and warm.
But think of all the homeless,
Who are desolate and forlorn.

They have no tree or Christmas lights,
Or somewhere cosy to lay their heads,
If they are lucky a cardboard box
Will be their Christmas bed.

Mary and Joseph may have been homeless
If the innkeeper had not let them stay
In his cold stable, dark and bare
Where Jesus was born the next day.

In our prayers let us remember,
As another Christmas is born,
All the homeless sleeping rough
On this year's Christmas morn.